Tiger Talk
All About Me

My Body

Leon Read

SEA-TO-SEA

Mankato Collingwood London

Contents

Look for Tiger on the pages of this book. Sometimes he is hiding.

We all have a body.

Body parts

Our bodies have a head, shoulders, knees, and toes, and eyes and ears and a mouth and a nose!

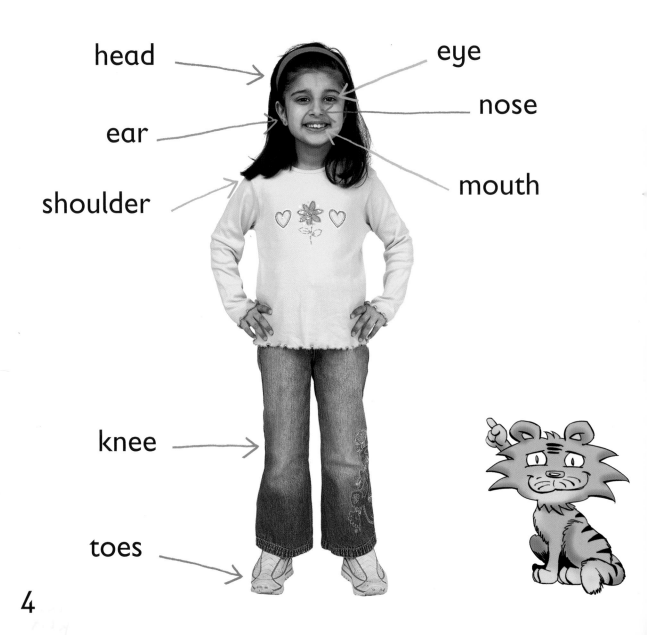

head

eye

nose

ear

mouth

shoulder

knee

toes

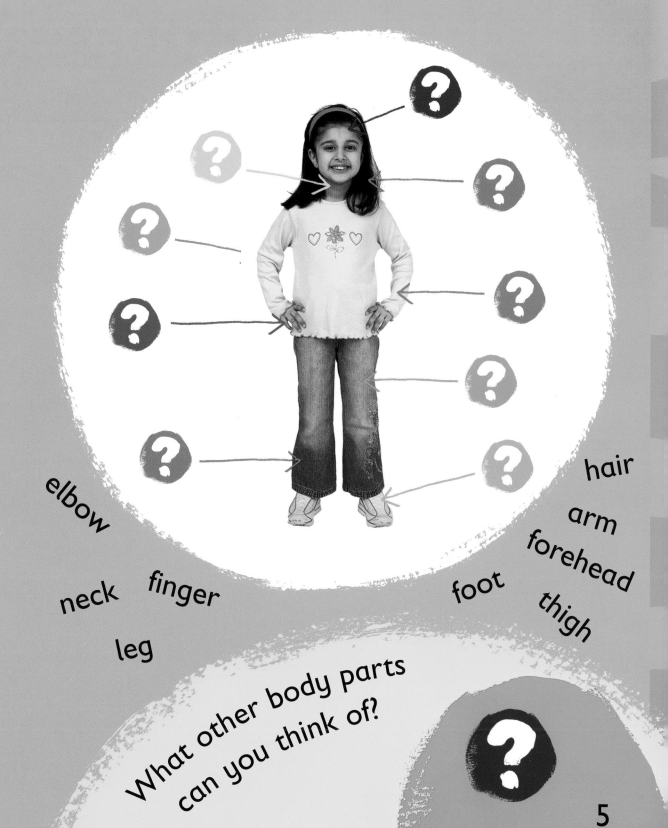

elbow

neck   finger

leg

hair

arm

forehead

foot   thigh

What other body parts can you think of?

Beautiful bodies

All of our bodies are different.

Use words like these
to describe your body.

brown eyes

black hair

round face

small ears

Using our body

We use our legs and feet to stand, walk, run, jump, and dance.

Grace has a wheelchair to help her move around.

What do you use all these body parts for?

nose

ear

eye

foot

hand

Body energy

We eat food to give our body energy.

What happens if we do not eat?

My stomach rumbles!

I get tired and grumpy.

Quick and still

We are playing a game called statues.

Our bodies can move very quickly.

Our bodies can stand very still.

Copy Charlie

1

2

3

5

4

Can you copy all of Charlie's hand shapes?

14

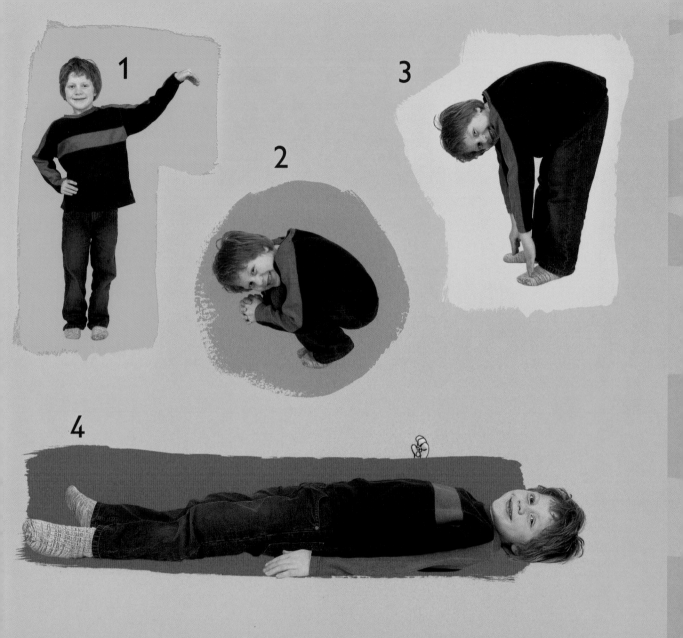

1

2

3

4

Can you copy all of Charlie's body shapes?

?

Hairy head

We have hair on our head.

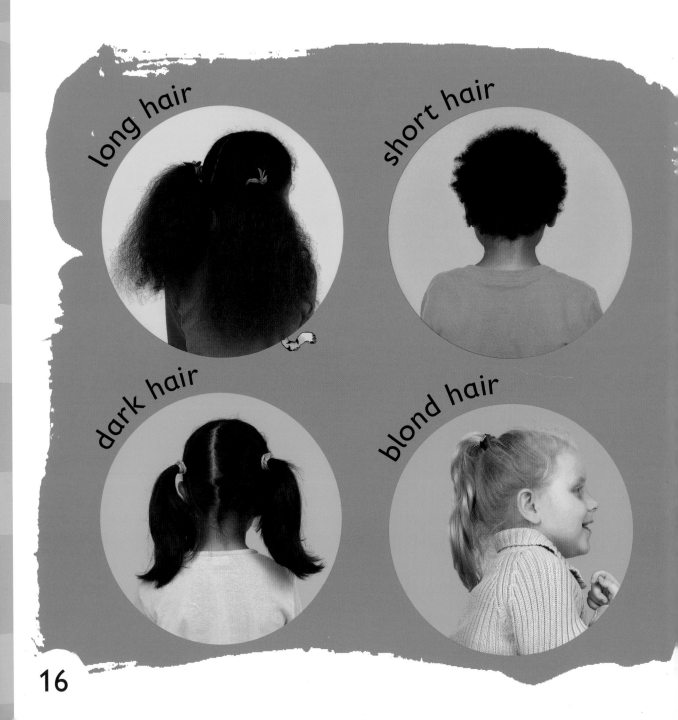

long hair

short hair

dark hair

blond hair

When hair is cut, it grows back.

Why does my dad have a hairy face?

How tall are you?

Young people are not very tall.

I can't reach!

I'm taller than my best friend, but I'm shorter than my older sister.

Measure your family. Ask for help if you cannot reach. Who is tallest?

Ouch! That hurts

Falling down can hurt.

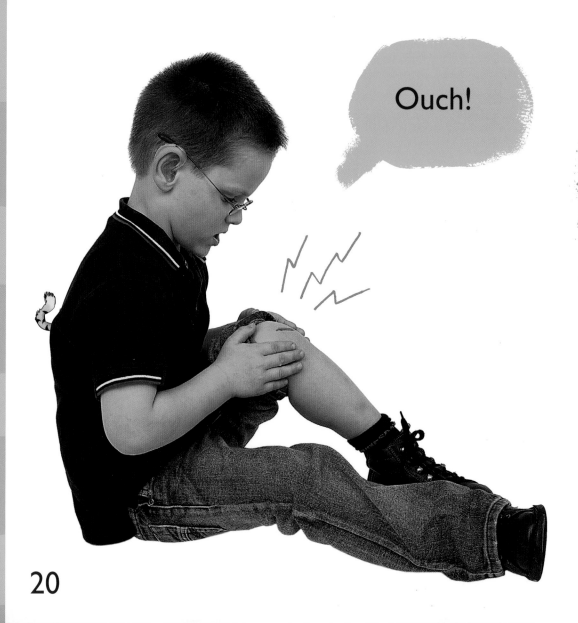

Ouch!

Billy has cut his knee.
I gave him a bandage.
It will help his knee
to get better.

All about me

Tiger has made a book about himself.

He included:

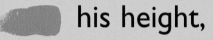 his height,

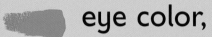 eye color,

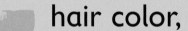 hair color,

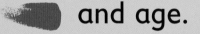 and age.

Height: 8 in (20 cm).

Eyes: black.

Fur: white and orange with black stripes.

Age: 4 years.

Look! I made a book and you can make one, too.

23

Word picture bank

Cut—P. 20

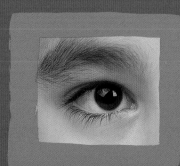

Eye—P. 4, 7, 9

Hair—P. 5, 7, 16, 17

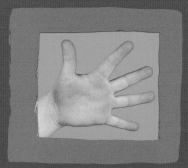

Hand—P. 9, 14

Hunger—P. 11

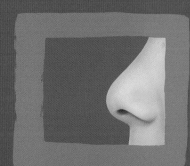

Nose—P. 4, 9

This edition first published in 2010 by Sea-to-Sea Publications
Distributed by Black Rabbit Books
P.O. Box 3263, Mankato, Minnesota 56002
Copyright © Sea-to-Sea Publications 2010

Printed in USA

All rights reserved.

9 8 7 6 5 4 3 2

Published by arrangement with the Watts Publishing Group
Ltd, London.

Library of Congress Cataloging-in-Publication Data
Read, Leon.
  My body / Leon Read.
    p. cm. -- (Tiger talk. All about me)
  Includes index.
  ISBN 978-1-59771-187-6 (hardcover)
  1. Human physiology--Juvenile literature. 2. Body, Human--Juvenile
literature. I. Title.
  QP37.M92 2010
  612--dc22
                           2008045009

Series editor: Adrian Cole

Photographer: Andy Crawford (unless otherwise credited)
Design: Sphere Design Associates
Art director: Jonathan Hair
Consultants: Prue Goodwin and Karina Law

Acknowledgments:
The Publisher would like to thank Norrie Carr model agency
and Scope. "Tiger" puppet used with kind permission from
Ravensden PLC (www.ravensden.co.uk).
Tiger Talk logo drawn by Kevin Hopgood.

(17t) © Bohemian Nomad
Picturemakers/Corbis.
(19) Lilly Dong/Botanica/
Jupiter Images.

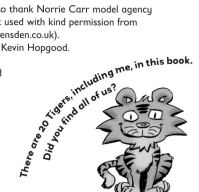

There are 20 Tigers, including me, in this book.
Did you find all of us?